Ember of Hope

Ember of Hope

Carina Schroedel

CONTENTS

About the Author

Carina Schroedel, CSW, LCADCA, is a Clinical Social Worker and licensed alcohol and drug counselor with over a decade of experience in the mental health and addiction recovery fields. As the founder of **Ember & Ease**, she blends evidence-based clinical practices with holistic healing approaches, such as yoga, meditation, and mindfulness, to support individuals in their recovery journey.

Having worked with clients in both outpatient therapy settings and inpatient rehab facilities, Carina is deeply committed to providing compassionate, trauma-informed care. Her approach is rooted in empathy, self-compassion, and the belief that healing is a lifelong journey. With her personal experience navigating life's challenges, including supporting a loved one through addiction and embracing her own path to self-healing,

Carina brings both professional expertise and heartfelt understanding to her work.

In addition to her clinical practice, Carina is passionate about educating and supporting fellow clinicians, empaths, and those in recovery. She is dedicated to creating resources, such as workbooks, meditations, and recovery tools, that empower others to live fulfilling lives beyond addiction.

When she's not working with clients or creating healing resources, Carina enjoys spending time with her two children, Mason and Leia, practicing yoga, and connecting with nature.

Introduction

Welcome to your journey of recovery.

By opening this workbook, you are taking a courageous step toward change and healing. Recovery is not a straightforward path; it is a deeply personal journey filled with ups and downs, moments of triumph, and opportunities for profound growth. This workbook is here to support you through every twist and turn.

Whether you are just starting your recovery, finding your way through it, or picking up the pieces after a setback, each step you take is significant. This workbook has been thoughtfully created to guide you with compassion and understanding, offering tools that many others have found helpful. Within these pages, you will discover exercises, journaling prompts, and reflections that encourage you to explore your strengths, acknowledge your challenges, and navigate your way to a healthier, more authentic self.

Recovery is not just about stopping an addictive behavior; it's about reclaiming your life in all its fullness. It's a journey toward finding peace within yourself, developing resilience, and building the skills you need to thrive. It invites you to understand who you are, why you have made certain choices, and how you can move forward from patterns that no longer serve you. You have the strength to transform your life, and this workbook will help you tap into that strength.

As you go through these pages, you will find:

- Supportive messages that remind you of your inherent strength and capability.
- Thoughtful exercises and journaling prompts that encourage reflection and processing.
- Practical tools to help you manage triggers and emotions as you heal.

- Resources and citations that provide additional guidance on your recovery journey.

As you work through this workbook, remember that healing takes time, and it's important to practice kindness toward yourself. Know that you are on a journey of self-discovery, healing, and transformation.

Together, let's begin this important journey. You are not alone.

1

Understanding Addiction and Recovery

What Is Addiction?

Addiction is not a simple choice or weakness. It is a complex and multifaceted condition that deeply impacts the mind, body, and spirit. Addiction often begins as a coping mechanism—an attempt to manage stress, pain, trauma, or feelings of emptiness. What may start as occasional use or engagement with a behavior can gradually evolve into a compulsion that feels impossible to escape.

At its core, addiction alters the brain's chemistry and functionality. Over time, the brain becomes rewired to crave the substance or behavior, learning to associate it with relief, comfort, or escape. The cycle deepens, with the need for more of the substance or behavior to achieve the same effect. Addiction thrives in the space between emotional suffering and the temporary relief that substances or behaviors provide. The more this cycle is repeated, the more entrenched it becomes.

But here's the truth: Addiction is not a moral failing. It's a health condition that can happen to anyone, regardless of their background, education, or environment. Understanding this distinction is an important step in shedding the shame and guilt that so often accompany addiction. It is also the first step toward recovery.

The Cycle of Addiction

Addiction follows a cycle that can be incredibly difficult to break, especially when the individual feels trapped within it. This cycle often looks like this:

1. **The Temptation to Use**: In moments of emotional pain, stress, or overwhelming feelings, the desire to escape or numb these emotions becomes powerful. The addictive behavior or substance feels like the only way to cope, and the cycle begins again.
2. **Bingeing or Engaging in the Behavior**: The individual engages in the addictive behavior, seeking relief or numbness. This brings temporary satisfaction but doesn't address the underlying issues.
3. **Consequences and Guilt**: Following the behavior, negative consequences arise—whether health-related, social, or emotional. This is often followed by guilt, shame, or feelings of powerlessness.
4. **The Cycle Continues**: The emotional pain caused by the consequences often leads to the desire for relief once more, continuing the cycle. The cycle repeats, deepening the hold addiction has on the individual.

Breaking this cycle requires more than just stopping the behavior. It requires self-awareness, self-compassion, and a commitment to healing, no matter how many setbacks you may encounter along the way.

What Is Recovery?

Recovery is not just about abstaining from an addictive substance or behavior. It is a process of reclaiming your life, rediscovering who you truly are, and healing from the emotional, physical, and psychological toll addiction has taken on you. Recovery is about transformation—about becoming the person you are meant to be, free from the chains of addiction.

Recovery is personal. It doesn't look the same for everyone, and that's okay. It's about finding your path, healing in your way, and embracing the challenges that come with it. Recovery is also about building a life that is not just sober but fulfilling, meaningful, and joyful.

At its heart, recovery is the act of choosing yourself. It is a commitment to your own well-being and future. It is a declaration that you are worthy of health, peace, and happiness.

The Stages of Recovery

Recovery is a process, not a destination. It unfolds in stages, each one bringing its own challenges and triumphs. Here are the typical stages of recovery:

1. **Precontemplation**: This is the stage where an individual may not yet recognize the problem or may be in denial. There may be resistance to acknowledging that addiction is a part of their life.
2. **Contemplation**: In this stage, the individual starts to become aware of the problem and begins to think about the possibility of recovery. There may be a sense of ambivalence—wanting change but also fearing it.

3. **Preparation**: The individual begins to take steps toward recovery, whether it's seeking help, setting goals, or planning their next move. There's a shift from contemplation to action.
4. **Action**: This is where the individual takes active steps to heal. They might enter treatment, start therapy, attend meetings, or adopt new coping strategies. This is often the most challenging stage, but it is also the most rewarding.
5. **Maintenance**: After initial success, recovery becomes about maintaining progress and managing potential setbacks. This stage requires ongoing commitment to self-care, healthy habits, and relapse prevention strategies.
6. **Relapse**: Relapse is a common part of recovery. It is not a failure but an opportunity for learning. If relapse happens, it doesn't mean you've failed; it means you have a chance to reassess and rebuild your commitment to recovery.

Each of these stages is a vital part of the process. Recovery takes time and dedication. Embrace where you are right now, knowing that each step forward is a victory.

Reflection Activity: What Does Recovery Mean to You?

Take a moment to reflect on what recovery means for you, personally. There's no right or wrong answer—your vision for recovery is uniquely yours.

- **What are your motivations for recovery?**
- **What would your life look like if you were free from addiction?**

- **What emotions, experiences, or outcomes do you hope to cultivate through recovery?**

Use the space below to write your thoughts:

Exercise: Identifying Your Personal Recovery Goals

Setting clear, achievable goals is an essential part of your recovery. Goals provide direction and help you measure your progress. The process of setting these goals should feel empowering—this is your journey, and you are in control.

Take time to think about what you want to focus on in your recovery. These goals might evolve over time, and that's okay. Begin by thinking about goals for the short term, medium term, and long term.

- **Immediate Goal (1 week):** What is one thing you can do right now to take a step toward recovery? (e.g., attend a support group, reach out for help, practice self-care)
- **Short-Term Goal (1 month):** What do you want to achieve in the next month? (e.g., stay sober, rebuild a relationship, establish a routine)
- **Long-Term Goal (6 months - 1 year):** What do you want your life to look like in the next six months to a year? (e.g., regain trust from loved ones, maintain a sober lifestyle, pursue personal dreams)

Write your goals below and reflect on how they can help guide you on your path:

- **Immediate Goal**:

- **Short-Term Goal**:
- **Long-Term Goal**:

2

Understanding Self-Compassion

The journey to recovery requires more than just overcoming the addictive behavior. It requires rebuilding the relationship you have with yourself. Self-compassion is the cornerstone of this process. It's not about perfection or self-indulgence—it's about showing yourself the kindness, patience, and understanding that you would offer to a loved one going through a tough time.

In a world that often encourages self-criticism and comparison, it can feel difficult to embrace self-compassion. We are taught to push ourselves harder, to be "tough" or "strong," and to minimize our feelings of pain or weakness. But in recovery, it's essential to challenge this mindset. You are not weak for needing help. You are not flawed for making mistakes. You are simply human. And being human means embracing both the light and shadow parts of yourself with love and care.

Self-compassion means giving yourself permission to be imperfect, to struggle, and to heal at your own pace. It is about replacing self-judgment with empathy, and offering yourself the grace that you deserve. When you practice self-compassion, you create a safe space within yourself to heal, to grow, and to rebuild. It allows you to acknowledge your mistakes without shame, to move through difficult emotions without self-blame, and to treat yourself with the same gentleness you would offer a friend or loved one.

Why Self-Compassion Matters in Recovery

Addiction thrives in an environment of self-criticism and shame. For many, the cycle of addiction is fueled by feelings of unworthiness or deep emotional pain. Without self-compassion, the emotional wounds that drive addiction often remain unhealed, leading to relapse and continued suffering.

Recovery requires you to dig deep into your emotional landscape, and it can be an overwhelming process. During these times, self-compassion is not a luxury—it's a necessity. It provides the emotional foundation for healing, allowing you to navigate the ups and downs of recovery with resilience and grace. It empowers you to face challenges with a mindset that fosters growth, rather than defeat.

Self-compassion helps you move from a place of self-loathing to self-acceptance. It's the antidote to guilt and shame, and it allows you to embrace both your triumphs and setbacks without judgment. By practicing self-compassion, you learn that you are worthy of recovery, worthy of love, and worthy of the life you are building.

How to Practice Self-Compassion

Practicing self-compassion involves changing the way you speak to yourself and how you respond to your emotions. It's about being gentle, patient, and understanding with yourself—just as you would be with a dear friend. Here are a few practical ways to start incorporating self-compassion into your daily life:

1. **Acknowledge Your Struggles Without Judgment**
When you face a setback or struggle, pause for a moment. Instead of criticizing yourself, acknowledge that you're experiencing difficulty, and remind yourself that it's okay. You are not defined by your challenges, but by how you move through them.
Example Affirmation: "I am doing the best I can right now, and it's okay to struggle. I will learn and grow from this experience."
2. **Speak to Yourself with Kindness**
When negative thoughts arise, challenge them. Ask yourself, "Would I say this to a friend who is struggling?" If not, then don't say it to yourself. Shift the language to something more compassionate and kind.
Example Affirmation: "I am worthy of kindness, even when I feel I don't deserve it."
3. **Allow Yourself to Feel Without Shame**
Emotions like sadness, frustration, or anger are part of being human. Self-compassion means accepting these emotions without suppressing or judging them. Allow yourself to feel what you're feeling and recognize that these emotions are temporary.
4. **Forgive Yourself**
Recovery is a journey, and there will be times when you make mistakes or feel as though you've failed. In those moments, practice self-forgiveness. Recognize that mistakes are a part of the process, not the end of the road.
5. **Create a Self-Compassion Ritual**
This might include things like taking a quiet moment for yourself, practicing deep breathing, or engaging in a comforting activity that brings you peace. Make time for yourself regularly—this is not indulgence; it's self-care.

Reflection Activity: Understanding Your Inner Critic

Take a moment to reflect on the way you speak to yourself, especially when you're struggling. Write down some of the critical or judgmental thoughts you've had recently. Now, imagine what you would say to a friend who shared these same struggles. What would you say to them?

Write down how you would offer compassion to a friend, and then practice offering that same kindness to yourself. This exercise can help you reframe your inner dialogue, shifting from self-criticism to self-compassion.

What would you say to a friend going through a tough time?

- Example: "You're doing the best you can. I'm so proud of your strength."

Now, write this message to yourself. What would it look like if you spoke to yourself with that same compassion?

- Example: "It's okay to be struggling right now. I'm proud of you for being so strong and committed to healing."

Exercise: Journaling to Cultivate Self-Compassion

Take a few minutes each day to journal about how you've shown yourself compassion. This could be a moment of self-kindness, a time when you forgave yourself, or a step you took to care for your emotional health.

- **Today, I showed myself compassion by...**
- **I forgive myself for...**

- **One thing I love about myself is...**

3

Building a Recovery Mindset

The Power of Your Mindset in Recovery

Your mindset is the lens through which you view the world, yourself, and your circumstances. In recovery, your mindset plays a pivotal role in determining your success. The way you think about addiction, healing, and your ability to overcome challenges can either hinder or propel you forward.

Building a recovery mindset means shifting from a fixed mindset, where you believe your abilities and circumstances are set in stone, to a growth mindset, where you understand that healing, change, and growth are always possible, regardless of where you've been or what you've been through. It's about moving from a place of "I can't" to "I can."

This shift doesn't happen overnight. It takes time, practice, and patience. However, cultivating a growth mindset will give you the strength to face the inevitable setbacks of recovery with resilience and the confidence to keep moving forward.

Fixed vs. Growth Mindset

1. **Fixed Mindset**: A person with a fixed mindset believes their traits, including their intelligence, abilities, and even recovery potential, are fixed and unchangeable. If they face failure or challenges, they see it as proof of their inability to succeed.
   Example Thought: "I've tried so many times before, and I always relapse. I'm just not strong enough."
2. **Growth Mindset**: A person with a growth mindset believes that they can develop their abilities through effort, learning, and persistence. They see setbacks as opportunities to learn and grow, rather than evidence of failure. In recovery, this mindset helps you stay committed even when things get difficult.
   Example Thought: "I've had setbacks, but I am capable of learning and making changes. Each step forward counts."

In recovery, a growth mindset is your ally. It helps you recognize that you are capable of change and that no mistake or setback defines you. Each moment is an opportunity to grow, to learn, and to become stronger.

The Role of Self-Talk in Shaping Your Mindset

The way you speak to yourself has a powerful impact on your mindset. Self-talk—the internal dialogue you have with yourself—can either reinforce negative beliefs or empower you to take positive action. The words you use in your mind can either help you rise above challenges or drag you down further into self-doubt.

Negative self-talk might sound like:

- "I'm a failure."
- "I'll never get through this."
- "I don't deserve a better life."

Positive self-talk can sound like:

- "I am learning and growing every day."
- "Setbacks are a part of recovery, not the end."
- "I am worthy of a healthy, fulfilling life."

In recovery, it's essential to challenge your negative self-talk and replace it with more compassionate, empowering statements. Positive affirmations can help reframe your thoughts and remind you of your inner strength.

Shifting Your Focus from Problems to Solutions

One of the most powerful shifts you can make in building a recovery mindset is moving from focusing on problems to focusing on solutions. It's easy to get lost in the challenges of addiction and recovery—the cravings, the triggers, the emotional rollercoaster. But when you focus only on the obstacles, it's hard to see the way forward.

In contrast, a solution-oriented mindset encourages you to identify ways to overcome difficulties. It's about asking yourself, "What can I do right now to move toward healing?" rather than getting stuck in the "I can't" thoughts.

For example, if you're feeling tempted to relapse, instead of focusing on how difficult it is to resist, try asking yourself:

- "What coping strategies can I use right now to calm myself down?"
- "Who can I reach out to for support?"
- "What small step can I take today to move closer to my goal of staying sober?"

By focusing on solutions, you take the power back and remind yourself that you are in control of your recovery.

The Importance of Patience and Persistence

In recovery, the road ahead is rarely a straight line. You will face setbacks, obstacles, and moments when things feel impossible. This is where patience and persistence come in. Building a recovery mindset means understanding that healing takes time. It's not about rushing the process or expecting immediate results—it's about showing up for yourself every day, no matter how hard it gets.

Each small step, no matter how insignificant it may seem in the moment, adds up. Healing happens bit by bit, one day at a time. Patience and persistence are your companions in this process.

Reflection Activity: Reframing Your Recovery Story

Take a moment to reflect on your journey. Consider the times when you've felt discouraged or defeated. Now, try to reframe those moments with a growth mindset. How can you look at those experiences as opportunities for learning and growth?

Write your reflections below:

- **When I struggled, I learned...**

- **A challenge I faced was... and I grew by...**
- **I am capable of recovery because...**

This exercise will help you shift from focusing on past failures to focusing on the lessons learned and the strength you've gained.

Exercise: Positive Affirmations for Recovery

Positive affirmations are a powerful way to shift your mindset and create a positive, empowering belief system. Each day, write down at least three affirmations that reinforce your belief in your recovery and your ability to overcome challenges.

Here are a few examples to get you started:

- "I am capable of overcoming any challenge that comes my way."
- "Every day is a step closer to the life I want to live."
- "I am worthy of love, health, and happiness."

Write your own affirmations below, and say them out loud every morning to set a positive tone for your day:

- **Affirmation 1**:
- **Affirmation 2**:
- **Affirmation 3**:

The Power of Visualization in Recovery

Visualization is a powerful tool for manifesting your recovery goals. Spend a few moments each day visualizing yourself living a life of recovery. Imagine yourself healthy, sober, and thriving. Picture the people you love, the activities that bring you joy, and the peace you feel in this new chapter of your life.

The more vivid and detailed your visualization, the more real it becomes. By imagining success, you reinforce the belief that recovery is not just possible, but already happening within you.

4

Emotional Awareness and Regulation

The Importance of Emotions in Recovery

Emotions are a fundamental part of being human, yet they can often feel overwhelming or difficult to navigate, especially during recovery. For many individuals struggling with addiction, emotions are at the root of their behaviors. Emotional distress—whether from stress, trauma, loneliness, or fear—often drives the need to escape through substances or compulsive behaviors. But emotions are not the enemy. In fact, understanding and learning to manage your emotions is one of the most powerful tools you have in recovery.

Addiction is often a coping mechanism for numbing or avoiding painful emotions. Over time, this coping strategy becomes automatic, and it can be difficult to find new ways to address feelings in a healthier way. Recovery, however, provides an opportunity to build emotional awareness and learn how to regulate these emotions without relying on substances or destructive behaviors.

Emotional awareness is the practice of recognizing, understanding, and accepting your emotions. It's about giving yourself permission to feel without judgment. Regulation, on the other hand, involves managing those emotions in a way that is constructive and healthy, rather than impulsively reacting or turning to harmful behaviors.

Understanding the Role of Emotions in Addiction

Many people who struggle with addiction have experienced emotional trauma, loss, or unmet needs that were never addressed. Emotions, particularly uncomfortable ones like sadness, anger, or anxiety, can be overwhelming and hard to face. Substances or addictive behaviors often offer temporary relief from these emotions, but they do not address the root causes.

In recovery, emotions will inevitably surface. This can be difficult at first, but it's important to remember that these feelings are normal. They are part of the healing process. The goal of recovery is not to avoid or suppress emotions but to understand them, express them in healthy ways, and use them as information to guide your growth.

Developing Emotional Awareness

Emotional awareness starts with acknowledging your feelings without judgment. It's easy to dismiss, suppress, or even criticize your emotions, especially if they feel uncomfortable or overwhelming. However, the first step to emotional regulation is simply noticing what you feel, naming it, and accepting that it is valid. All emotions, whether positive or negative, are a natural part of the human experience. They are signals that inform us about our inner world.

Start by practicing mindfulness, which helps you stay present with your emotions and prevents you from being swept away by them. Mindfulness teaches you to notice emotions as they arise and to allow them to be present without rushing to change them. You don't have to "fix" or "get rid of" emotions; you just need to sit with them for a moment and allow them to exist.

Emotional Awareness Exercise: Identifying Your Feelings

Take a few moments each day to sit quietly and check in with yourself. Ask yourself:

- What emotions am I feeling right now?
- Where do I feel this emotion in my body?
- What might be triggering this emotion?

You can use a feelings wheel or list to help identify emotions you may not be familiar with. Some emotions might feel complicated or multi-layered, and that's okay. Just focus on recognizing what is present without judgment.

Emotional Regulation Tools

Once you have begun to identify and understand your emotions, the next step is learning how to regulate them. Emotional regulation does not mean suppressing emotions or pretending they don't exist. Instead, it involves finding ways to manage your emotional responses in healthy, constructive ways.

Here are several techniques to help you regulate your emotions:

1. **Deep Breathing**

   When you're feeling overwhelmed, one of the quickest ways to bring yourself back to a balanced state is through deep breathing. Slow, intentional breathing helps activate the body's relaxation response and can reduce feelings of anxiety, anger, or sadness.

   How to Practice:

- Sit comfortably with your feet flat on the ground.
- Close your eyes and inhale deeply through your nose for a count of four.
- Hold your breath for a count of four.
- Slowly exhale through your mouth for a count of six.
- Repeat this for several minutes.

2. **Progressive Muscle Relaxation (PMR)**

Progressive muscle relaxation is a technique where you tense and then release different muscle groups in your body. This helps release physical tension and can have a calming effect on your mind as well.

How to Practice:

- Find a comfortable place to sit or lie down.
- Begin by tensing the muscles in your feet for 5 seconds, then release them for 10 seconds.
- Gradually move up your body, tensing and releasing each muscle group (legs, abdomen, chest, arms, neck, face).
- Focus on the sensation of relaxation after each release.

3. **Mindful Journaling**

Journaling is a powerful tool for emotional regulation. Writing down your feelings allows you to process and release emotions, gain perspective, and reflect on your progress. Journaling can also help you identify patterns in your emotional responses and develop healthier coping strategies over time.

How to Practice:

- Set aside time each day to write freely about your emotions.

- Start with prompts like, "Today I'm feeling..." or "The most difficult part of my day was..."
- Write for at least 10 minutes without judgment, letting your thoughts flow onto the page.

4. **Grounding Techniques**

Grounding exercises help you stay in the present moment and calm overwhelming emotions. These techniques bring your attention to your surroundings and the present reality, helping to break the cycle of spiraling negative thoughts.

How to Practice:

- 5-4-3-2-1 Grounding Exercise: Notice and name 5 things you can see, 4 things you can touch, 3 things you can hear, 2 things you can smell, and 1 thing you can taste. This brings you into your body and helps reconnect with the present moment.

Reflection Activity: Reflecting on Your Emotional Triggers

Take some time to reflect on your emotional triggers. Write down a few situations that tend to trigger intense emotional reactions for you. These could be things like specific people, stress at work, or memories of past trauma. Next, think about how you've responded in the past. Were there healthier ways you could have responded? What can you do next time to regulate your emotions more effectively?

Emotional Trigger:

Reaction:

Healthier Response:

Exercise: Developing Your Own Emotional Regulation Plan

Create a plan for how you will respond the next time you feel overwhelmed by emotions. Think about the tools you've learned in this chapter and choose the ones that resonate with you most. Write down your plan and keep it with you as a reminder.

When I feel overwhelmed, I will...

- Practice deep breathing for 5 minutes.
- Use the 5-4-3-2-1 grounding exercise.
- Write about my emotions in my journal.
- Reach out to my support system.

5

Developing Healthy Coping Strategies

Why Healthy Coping Matters in Recovery

Coping mechanisms are the tools we use to deal with stress, discomfort, and difficult emotions. In addiction, unhealthy coping mechanisms, such as substance use, have often been used to numb or escape emotional pain. Recovery, however, requires replacing these harmful coping strategies with healthier alternatives that promote healing and growth.

Healthy coping strategies not only help manage the day-to-day stressors of life but also build resilience—the ability to bounce back from setbacks, face challenges with strength, and maintain your commitment to recovery. Building these strategies is not a quick fix, but rather a gradual process of learning new skills and behaviors that support emotional well-being.

Research has shown that individuals who have developed healthy coping strategies are better equipped to handle stress, regulate their emotions, and avoid relapse. According to Dr. Marsha Linehan, creator of Dialectical Behavior Therapy (DBT), "Skills are the bridge between knowledge and action" (Linehan, 1993). In other words, the coping strategies you develop today will empower you to act with resilience in the face of future challenges.

In this chapter, we will explore a range of coping techniques designed to support you in managing stress, regulating emotions, and maintaining your progress in recovery.

Understanding Your Triggers

Before developing new coping strategies, it's important to understand your personal triggers—those situations, people, or emotions that lead to cravings or the urge to use substances. Triggers can be external (such as stressful situations or certain environments) or internal (such as negative emotions like anxiety or loneliness). Identifying these triggers gives you the power to recognize when they arise and use coping strategies to manage them effectively.

Dr. Gabor Maté, a renowned addiction expert, explains, "The opposite of addiction is not sobriety. The opposite of addiction is connection" (Maté, 2008). In other words, when we feel emotionally connected and supported, we are less likely to turn to harmful behaviors for relief. Understanding your triggers and how they connect to deeper emotional needs can help you find healthier ways to cope.

Healthy Coping Strategies to Manage Stress and Emotions

1. **Mindfulness and Meditation**
   Mindfulness is the practice of being fully present in the moment, without judgment. Research has shown that mindfulness and meditation are powerful tools for reducing stress, improving emotional regulation, and preventing relapse. These practices allow you to observe your thoughts and feelings without reacting im-

pulsively, helping you build greater emotional awareness and resilience.

How to Practice:

- Find a quiet, comfortable space.
- Close your eyes and focus on your breath. Inhale deeply through your nose, hold for a moment, then exhale slowly.
- Allow your thoughts to come and go without judgment, gently bringing your focus back to your breath whenever your mind wanders.
- Start with 5 minutes a day and gradually increase the time as you feel comfortable.

Professional Insight:

"Mindfulness allows us to break free from the automaticity of our habits, to create a gap between stimulus and reaction." – Dr. Jon Kabat-Zinn, founder of Mindfulness-Based Stress Reduction (Kabat-Zinn, 1990).

2. **Exercise and Physical Activity**

Physical activity is a natural and effective way to release stress, boost mood, and promote overall well-being. Regular exercise releases endorphins, the body's natural "feel-good" chemicals, which can help reduce anxiety and improve your mental clarity. Exercise also helps you build physical resilience, which is essential for long-term recovery.

How to Practice:

- Start with a form of exercise that feels enjoyable—whether it's walking, yoga, swimming, or dancing.

- Aim for at least 30 minutes of physical activity most days of the week.
- Choose activities that help you connect with your body and promote a sense of accomplishment.

Professional Insight:
"Exercise is the most potent tool we have for improving mental health." – Dr. John Ratey, author of *Spark: The Revolutionary New Science of Exercise and the Brain* (Ratey, 2008).

3. **Journaling for Emotional Release**

Journaling is a powerful tool for emotional expression and reflection. Writing down your thoughts and feelings allows you to process emotions that might be difficult to express verbally. Journaling helps you gain perspective, release negative emotions, and explore solutions to challenges.

How to Practice:

- Set aside 10-15 minutes each day to write about your thoughts, feelings, and experiences.
- Use prompts like, "What am I feeling right now?" or "What challenges did I face today and how did I cope?"
- Allow yourself to write freely, without judgment, and let the words flow.

Professional Insight:
"Writing helps us sort out our thoughts, relieve stress, and improve our mental health." – Dr. James Pennebaker, Professor of Psychology, University of Texas, author of *Opening Up* (Pennebaker, 1997).

4. **Breathing Exercises for Calm and Clarity**

When you feel overwhelmed, one of the quickest ways to calm your nervous system is through deep breathing exercises. Deep breathing activates the body's parasympathetic nervous system, which helps counteract the effects of stress and anxiety.

How to Practice:

- Inhale deeply for a count of 4, hold for a count of 4, and exhale slowly for a count of 6.
- Focus on your breath and feel your body relax with each exhale.
- Practice deep breathing whenever you feel triggered or stressed.

Professional Insight:

"Breathing exercises are one of the most effective ways to shift the body out of a state of stress and into a state of relaxation." – Dr. Andrew Weil, author of *Spontaneous Healing* (Weil, 1995).

5. **Building a Support Network**

Recovery is not a solitary journey—it requires connection and support. Building a strong support network of friends, family, or recovery groups can provide emotional support, accountability, and encouragement when you need it most. The relationships you nurture in recovery will help reinforce your commitment to change and provide comfort during difficult times.

How to Practice:

- Reach out to someone you trust whenever you're feeling overwhelmed or tempted to relapse.

- ◦ Consider joining a support group like Narcotics Anonymous (NA) or Alcoholics Anonymous (AA), where you can share your journey with others who understand.
- ◦ Surround yourself with people who lift you up and support your recovery.

Professional Insight:

"The more people we involve in our healing, the more we have to learn and the better equipped we are to stay well." – Dr. Brene Brown, researcher and author of *The Gifts of Imperfection* (Brown, 2010).

Reflection Activity: Identifying Your Coping Strategies

Take a moment to reflect on how you have historically coped with stress and difficult emotions. Write down some of the coping strategies you have used in the past, both healthy and unhealthy. Now, think about how you can replace the unhealthy strategies with the healthy ones discussed in this chapter.

Past Coping Strategies:

- Unhealthy:
- Healthy:

Exercise: Building Your Coping Toolbox

Create a toolbox of healthy coping strategies that resonate with you. These can be techniques from this chapter or new ideas you've discovered on your own. The goal is to have a variety of tools at your disposal for different emotional situations.

Write down the strategies you can use when you feel stressed, anxious, or triggered:

- **When I feel stressed, I will...**
- **When I feel triggered, I will...**
- **When I feel sad, I will...**

Building Resilience Through Coping

As you build and refine your coping toolbox, remember that it's not about being perfect—it's about progress. Recovery is about learning and growing, and the more tools you have at your disposal, the better equipped you'll be to handle the challenges of life. Each time you choose a healthy coping strategy over an unhealthy one, you are reinforcing your commitment to your well-being and your future.

6

Understanding Trauma and Its Role in Addiction

The Link Between Trauma and Addiction

Trauma is often a hidden force in addiction. It can stem from many different experiences—abuse, neglect, loss, violence, or significant life stressors—and it can leave deep emotional scars that affect how we view ourselves and the world around us. For many individuals in recovery, unresolved trauma is a key factor that perpetuates addictive behaviors.

Addiction can be seen as a coping mechanism for managing emotional pain caused by trauma. Whether through substances, compulsive behaviors, or other forms of escapism, addiction offers a temporary way to numb the intense feelings associated with past experiences. Unfortunately, while addiction may offer short-term relief, it never addresses the root cause of the pain. This is why understanding and healing from trauma is a crucial part of the recovery process.

Dr. Gabor Maté, a leading expert in addiction and trauma, says, "The question is not why the addiction, but why the pain?" (Maté, 2008). Addiction is often the answer to the emotional wounds that trauma leaves behind. In order to recover fully, healing these wounds is essential.

Types of Trauma and Their Impact

Trauma can take many forms, both visible and invisible. It's important to recognize the various types of trauma and how they may have influenced your life and addiction.

1. **Physical and Sexual Abuse**
   Physical or sexual abuse can have long-lasting effects on the mind and body. Survivors of abuse often struggle with low self-worth, fear, and trust issues, all of which can contribute to the development of addictive behaviors as a way to cope with the emotional fallout.
2. **Emotional and Psychological Abuse**
   Emotional abuse, such as constant criticism, rejection, or manipulation, can leave deep scars. It often results in feelings of shame, anxiety, and depression, leading individuals to seek relief through substances or addictive behaviors.
3. **Neglect**
   Childhood neglect, whether physical, emotional, or both, can cause profound feelings of abandonment and loneliness. These feelings can manifest in addiction as a way to fill the emotional void left by neglectful caregiving.
4. **Loss and Grief**
   Loss of a loved one, whether through death, separation, or other means, can trigger deep emotional pain. Unresolved grief can lead to a desire to numb the pain, often leading individuals to turn to substances or behaviors to avoid feeling the loss.

5. **Complex Trauma**
   Complex trauma refers to ongoing or repeated traumatic experiences, such as living in a violent home or being part of an abusive relationship. It results in a wide range of emotional and psychological challenges, including difficulty with emotional regulation, relationships, and trust.

Recognizing the impact of trauma on addiction is the first step in healing. It allows you to understand that your addiction is not just a matter of willpower, but rather a response to deep emotional pain. This understanding can help break the cycle of shame and self-blame that often accompanies both trauma and addiction.

The Role of Trauma in Addiction and Recovery

Understanding trauma's impact on addiction is crucial for recovery. Trauma can affect how you think, feel, and behave, often influencing your choices in ways that you may not even be aware of. For many, trauma shapes how they cope with stress, manage relationships, and view the world. It can lead to patterns of behavior that are harmful, such as addiction.

The journey to healing involves not just addressing the addiction itself, but also healing the trauma that may have contributed to it. This is where trauma-informed care becomes vital. **Trauma-informed care** is a treatment approach that recognizes the presence of trauma symptoms and acknowledges the role trauma plays in the lives of individuals seeking help.

Dr. Bessel van der Kolk, a renowned trauma researcher, emphasizes the importance of treating trauma in recovery: "The body keeps the score" (van der Kolk, 2014). Trauma is stored in the body, and the body's response to that trauma often manifests in addictive behaviors, physical ailments, and emotional struggles. Healing from trauma requires addressing both the emotional and physical effects it has on the body.

Healing Trauma in Recovery

Healing from trauma in recovery is a gradual and ongoing process. It requires compassion, patience, and the willingness to confront the pain of the past. While this process may feel overwhelming, it is also an opportunity for deep transformation and growth. There are several tools and approaches that can help individuals heal from trauma while in recovery:

1. **Therapeutic Approaches to Trauma Healing**

    - **Cognitive Behavioral Therapy (CBT)**: CBT helps individuals identify and change negative thought patterns that may have developed as a result of trauma. It can help individuals break free from the cycle of shame and guilt associated with both trauma and addiction.
    - **Trauma-Focused Cognitive Behavioral Therapy (TF-CBT)**: This specialized form of CBT is specifically designed to help individuals process trauma and develop healthier coping mechanisms.
    - **Somatic Therapy**: Somatic therapy focuses on the connection between the body and mind. It recognizes that trauma is stored in the body and that physical techniques, such as breathwork, movement, and touch, can help release trauma and promote healing.
    - **EMDR (Eye Movement Desensitization and Reprocessing)**: EMDR is a form of psychotherapy that helps in-

dividuals process traumatic memories through guided eye movements. It has been shown to be highly effective in reducing the emotional charge of traumatic memories.

2. **Building Emotional Resilience**
   - **Mindfulness**: Mindfulness practices, such as meditation and body awareness, help individuals stay present with their emotions, reducing the tendency to dissociate or numb painful memories. Mindfulness helps individuals process emotions in real-time without turning to substances for relief.
   - **Self-Compassion**: As discussed in Chapter 2, self-compassion is a key element in healing trauma. Being kind and gentle with yourself allows you to create a safe emotional space in which to process difficult feelings and memories without shame.
   - **Grounding Exercises**: Grounding techniques, such as deep breathing or the 5-4-3-2-1 method, help individuals stay connected to the present moment, reducing the overwhelming effects of traumatic memories.
3. **Building Trusting Relationships**
   - **Support Groups**: Peer support through 12-step programs like Alcoholics Anonymous (AA) or Narcotics Anonymous (NA) can provide a sense of community and connection. These groups offer individuals a space to share their experiences, support one another, and find solidarity in recovery.
   - **Therapeutic Relationships**: Developing a trusting relationship with a therapist or counselor is essential for

trauma healing. This relationship provides a safe space where you can explore your past experiences and begin to heal.

Reflection Activity: Identifying the Role of Trauma in Your Addiction

Take some time to reflect on the trauma you have experienced and how it may have influenced your addiction. Use the following questions to guide your reflections:

- **What traumatic experiences in my life might have contributed to my addiction?**
- **How have I coped with emotional pain in the past?**
- **What patterns do I notice in my life that are tied to unresolved trauma?**

Write your reflections below:

Exercise: Healing Through Compassionate Awareness

Healing trauma requires not only processing the pain but also acknowledging the deep emotional wounds that have shaped your addiction. One way to begin this process is through compassionate awareness. Start by sitting quietly, focusing on your breath, and bringing to mind a traumatic event or experience. Gently acknowledge the pain associated with it, offering yourself kindness and understanding as you sit with the memory. You are not defined by your past, but by how you choose to heal from it.

Write down your thoughts and feelings after this exercise:

- **How did it feel to sit with this memory?**
- **What can I do today to begin healing this trauma?**

Moving Forward: Trauma as Part of Your Healing Story

Healing from trauma is not a linear process. There will be moments of discomfort, but there will also be moments of profound growth and understanding. Your trauma does not define you, but your ability to heal from it does. By addressing the emotional pain and the root causes of your addiction, you are taking an empowering step toward a brighter, more fulfilling future.

7

Forgiveness and Letting Go

The Power of Forgiveness in Recovery

Forgiveness is often misunderstood. Many people believe that to forgive means to condone or excuse the behavior of others, but in reality, forgiveness is a powerful act of self-liberation. It's about releasing the hold that past hurt and anger have over you, not for the benefit of those who hurt you, but for your own peace and freedom.

In the context of recovery, forgiveness is essential. Holding onto anger, resentment, and bitterness can weigh heavily on your emotional health, keeping you tethered to the past and preventing you from fully embracing the present and future. It can fuel cycles of self-punishment and self-sabotage, both of which are detrimental to your well-being and your recovery journey.

Maya Angelou beautifully captured the transformative power of forgiveness: "Forgiveness is the greatest gift you can give yourself. It's not for the other person, it's for you" (Angelou, 1993). By choosing to forgive, you are choosing to free yourself from the emotional chains that bind you to your pain. You are taking control of your emotional health and your future.

Forgiveness of Others

Forgiving others who have wronged or hurt you may feel like an insurmountable challenge. Often, the wounds inflicted by others—whether through abuse, neglect, betrayal, or abandonment—can run deep. The anger and hurt that result from these experiences can linger for years, creating emotional barriers that make healing difficult.

However, holding onto these feelings of anger and resentment can be toxic. It is exhausting to carry around the weight of past grievances, and it limits your ability to experience peace and joy in the present. Forgiveness, in this case, is not about excusing the behavior of others—it's about freeing yourself from the burden of holding onto that anger and pain.

Forgiveness in recovery doesn't mean that what happened was okay, nor does it mean that you have to reconcile with the person who hurt you. It simply means that you are releasing the hold that their actions have on your life, allowing you to heal and move forward.

Dr. Frederic Luskin, the author of *Forgive for Good*, writes: "Forgiveness is the process of letting go of the past, and this act of letting go allows you to take control of your own life and your own future" (Luskin, 2002). By forgiving others, you reclaim your power and your ability to choose a path toward peace.

Forgiveness of Yourself

Perhaps the most challenging form of forgiveness is forgiving yourself. Shame and guilt are common emotional burdens for those in recovery. You may struggle with feelings of regret about past actions or decisions, believing that you are unworthy of love or forgiveness. These feelings can create a toxic cycle of self-blame, preventing you from fully engaging in your recovery journey.

In recovery, forgiving yourself is an essential step in healing. It is the act of releasing the shame and guilt that have kept you trapped in the past. It is acknowledging that you made mistakes but that those mistakes do not define you. You are not your past, and you are worthy of love and compassion, just as you are.

Tara Brach, a psychologist and meditation teacher, states, "True forgiveness does not mean excusing what happened; it means freeing yourself from the pain" (Brach, 2003). Self-forgiveness involves treating yourself with kindness and compassion, accepting that you are human and that healing is a process. You don't have to be perfect to be worthy of love and forgiveness—you only need to be willing to let go of the guilt and embrace the possibility of change.

The Process of Forgiveness

Forgiveness is not a one-time event—it is a process, and like recovery itself, it requires time, patience, and effort. It's important to approach forgiveness with the understanding that it may take time for the emotional wounds to heal. You may find that forgiveness is a continual practice, something you return to as you move through different stages of your recovery.

Here are some steps that can help guide you through the forgiveness process:

1. **Acknowledge the Hurt**
   Before you can forgive, you must first acknowledge the hurt and pain you've experienced. Denying or suppressing these emotions will only prolong the healing process. Give yourself permission to feel the pain, and allow yourself to express the emotions that arise without judgment.

2. **Understand the Impact of Holding Onto Resentment**
Reflect on the toll that anger, bitterness, or regret is taking on your emotional and physical well-being. Holding onto resentment can increase stress, anxiety, and even physical health problems. Recognize that by holding onto these negative emotions, you are allowing them to control your life, rather than releasing them for your own healing.
3. **Make the Choice to Forgive**
Forgiveness is ultimately a choice. It is about deciding that you no longer want to carry the burden of past hurt. This doesn't mean that you forget or condone what happened, but it does mean that you are choosing to release the hold that anger and resentment have over you.
4. **Practice Self-Compassion**
As you move through the process of forgiveness, practice self-compassion. Understand that it's okay to take time, that healing isn't linear, and that it's normal to experience setbacks. Be kind to yourself as you navigate this challenging but transformative process.
5. **Letting Go and Moving Forward**
Once you've made the choice to forgive, work on letting go of the emotional attachment to the hurt. This is where true healing begins. You don't need to carry the past with you anymore. By letting go of the anger and resentment, you open yourself to new possibilities—peace, joy, and freedom.

Reflection Activity: Who Do You Need to Forgive?

Forgiveness is a personal decision, and it can sometimes take time to process. Take a moment to reflect on who you may need to forgive in your life. This might include family members, friends, or even yourself.

Write down the names of those individuals and the reasons why forgiveness is difficult for you.

- **Who do I need to forgive?**
- **What pain or hurt am I holding onto?**
- **What would it feel like to forgive them?**
- **What is one small step I can take toward forgiveness today?**

Exercise: Writing a Letter of Forgiveness

One powerful exercise in forgiveness is writing a letter to someone who has hurt you. This letter does not need to be sent—it is simply a tool for processing your emotions and releasing the pain. Write the letter with honesty and openness, expressing your feelings and letting go of the hold that anger has on you.

- **To [Name],**
- **I forgive you for...**
- **I release the hold that this pain has had on me...**
- **I choose to let go and heal...**

Forgiving Yourself: A Guided Meditation

Forgiving yourself can often be the hardest part of the healing process. Take some time to sit in a quiet, comfortable space. Close your eyes and take a few deep breaths. Imagine yourself surrounded by warmth and light, offering yourself the kindness and compassion that you need.

Repeat the following affirmations to yourself:

- "I forgive myself for the mistakes I have made."
- "I release the shame and guilt that I've been holding onto."
- "I am worthy of love, peace, and healing."
- "I choose to move forward with compassion and grace."

The Freedom in Letting Go

Forgiveness is not a one-time act—it is an ongoing practice that will evolve as you continue on your recovery journey. As you release the emotional baggage of the past, you make room for healing, joy, and peace in the present. By forgiving yourself and others, you free yourself from the chains of resentment and allow your spirit to grow, to thrive, and to be reborn.

Remember, forgiveness is a gift you give to yourself, one that will carry you forward into a future filled with possibility and healing.

8

Rebuilding Relationships

The Impact of Addiction on Relationships

Addiction is not an isolated experience. It ripples outward, affecting every relationship in its path. Family, friends, colleagues, and romantic partners often bear the emotional weight of addiction, whether through enabling behaviors, emotional distance, or feelings of betrayal. As a result, the recovery process must include healing the relationships that have been strained or damaged by addiction.

For many individuals in recovery, the relationship with their loved ones is a primary source of support and motivation. However, rebuilding these connections can be one of the most challenging aspects of recovery. Trust has often been broken, and the emotional pain can feel insurmountable. However, rebuilding relationships is essential for creating a solid foundation for long-term recovery. Without healthy relationships, the journey toward healing can feel isolating and incomplete.

Dr. Stephanie Covington, a leading expert in women's recovery, states, "Recovery is not just about the individual—it's about rebuilding the relationships that support your growth and well-being" (Covington, 2008). The process of mending relationships is about reconnecting, rebuilding trust, and learning to communicate openly and honestly.

Rebuilding Trust

Trust is the cornerstone of any healthy relationship, and in recovery, rebuilding trust takes time and consistent effort. It is common for individuals in recovery to have damaged trust with family members, partners, and friends due to lies, broken promises, or erratic behavior. Rebuilding that trust is not something that happens overnight, but it is possible with patience, accountability, and transparency.

Here are a few ways to rebuild trust:

1. **Be Honest and Transparent**
   One of the first steps in rebuilding trust is committing to honesty. Recovery requires you to be open about your thoughts, feelings, and behaviors, even when it's difficult. This may mean admitting to past mistakes or failures and apologizing for the hurt caused.
   Professional Insight:
   "Trust is built through consistent, reliable actions over time. It's not about grand gestures, but small, daily actions that show commitment to change" – Dr. Jennifer J. Freyd, author of *Betrayal Trauma* (Freyd, 1996).
2. **Be Accountable for Your Actions**
   Accountability is a key part of rebuilding trust. This means not only acknowledging your past behavior but also taking responsibility for how it affected others. Being accountable shows that you are committed to change and willing to make amends.
3. **Apologize and Make Amends**
   A sincere apology is an important step in healing. It's about taking responsibility for your actions, expressing regret for the hurt you've caused, and asking for forgiveness. An apology is not about

justifying your actions but acknowledging the pain that your addiction has caused.

Dr. Brené Brown writes, "An apology is not about being right; it's about recognizing the impact of your actions and expressing regret for the pain it caused" (Brown, 2008).

4. **Be Patient**

   Trust takes time to rebuild. Your loved ones may need time to process the hurt and begin trusting you again. Be patient with them and with yourself. Show through your actions that you are committed to change, even if it takes time for trust to be fully restored.

Setting Healthy Boundaries

In recovery, healthy boundaries are essential for protecting your emotional well-being and maintaining your sobriety. During addiction, boundaries are often blurred or non-existent. The ability to set boundaries in relationships is critical to maintaining balance and avoiding enabling behaviors. Learning how to say no, assert your needs, and create safe spaces for yourself allows you to engage with others in a healthy and sustainable way.

Boundaries are not about creating walls between you and others—they are about creating the space needed for mutual respect and healthy interaction.

1. **Recognize Your Needs**

   Before you can set boundaries, you need to understand your own needs. Take time to reflect on what is important to you—your physical, emotional, and mental well-being—and what behaviors are not acceptable in your relationships.

2. **Learn to Say No**
   Saying no is a powerful tool for self-care. Whether it's declining an invitation to drink or asserting that you need time for yourself, learning to say no with confidence and compassion is essential for recovery. Boundaries are not about rejecting others; they are about protecting your own peace and growth.
3. **Communicate Clearly and Respectfully**
   Setting boundaries requires clear and respectful communication. It's important to express your needs directly, without apology or guilt. Be honest about what you need in relationships and how you expect to be treated.

   Professional Insight:
   "Healthy boundaries are the key to healthy relationships. Boundaries are the structure that allows love and respect to flourish" – Dr. Henry Cloud, author of *Boundaries* (Cloud, 1992).
4. **Respect Others' Boundaries**
   Just as it's important to set boundaries for yourself, it's equally important to respect the boundaries of others. Healthy relationships are built on mutual respect. Be mindful of the emotional needs and limits of those you are rebuilding relationships with.

Nurturing Meaningful Connections

In recovery, relationships can become sources of strength and support. Building new, healthy relationships and nurturing old ones is an essential part of the recovery process. However, it's important to recognize that not all relationships are supportive or conducive to your well-being. Part of your healing journey is learning how to surround yourself with people who genuinely support your recovery and growth.

Here's how to nurture meaningful connections:

1. **Seek Out Supportive People**
   In recovery, it's vital to surround yourself with people who encourage your growth and understand the challenges you face. Support groups, recovery meetings, and therapy can all offer a safe space to build new connections with people who are on a similar journey.
2. **Rebuild Your Social Circle**
   As you rebuild your life in recovery, it may be necessary to reevaluate your social circle. This might mean distancing yourself from individuals who enable addictive behaviors or who do not support your recovery. Surround yourself with people who inspire you to grow, live authentically, and stay committed to your sobriety.
3. **Invest Time in Healthy Relationships**
   Nurturing meaningful relationships requires effort. Make time for the people who matter to you—whether through regular check-ins, spending quality time together, or offering your support in return. Healthy relationships are built on trust, open communication, and mutual care.
4. **Be Open to New Connections**
   Recovery opens the door to new experiences and relationships. Embrace the opportunity to meet people who share your values and are aligned with your recovery goals. Whether through social activities, hobbies, or volunteering, there are countless ways to connect with others in meaningful ways.

Reflection Activity: Healing the Relationships You Value

Think about the relationships that have been impacted by your addiction. Which ones would you like to heal and rebuild? What steps can you take to restore trust and establish healthy boundaries?

- **Which relationships in my life need healing?**
- **What is one action I can take today to begin rebuilding trust?**
- **What boundaries do I need to set to protect my recovery?**

Exercise: Writing a Letter to Someone You've Hurt

Take a moment to write a letter to someone whose trust you've broken or whose pain you've caused. This letter is for your own healing, not necessarily to be sent. Express your regret and acknowledge the impact of your actions. Even if you're not ready to have this conversation with the person, this exercise will help you process the emotions involved in healing.

- **Dear [Name],**
- **I recognize the hurt I caused...**
- **I am committed to making things right...**
- **I ask for your forgiveness and hope that, in time, we can rebuild our relationship.**

The Journey of Healing Relationships

Rebuilding relationships is one of the most profound aspects of recovery. As you rebuild trust, set boundaries, and nurture meaningful connections, you are creating a strong foundation for a healthier, more fulfilling life. Remember that healing relationships takes time, and every step you take toward healing and growth is a step closer to a life of recovery that is rich with love, support, and connection.

9

Creating a Healthy Daily Routine

The Importance of Routine in Recovery

In the early stages of recovery, one of the most important things you can do for yourself is create a stable, healthy routine. Addiction often thrives in chaos, and without structure, it's easy to fall back into old habits or find yourself feeling overwhelmed by the demands of daily life. A healthy routine provides a sense of stability, reduces stress, and helps you stay focused on your recovery goals.

Establishing a routine gives you a sense of control and purpose. It can also create a buffer between you and the triggers or cravings that might arise throughout the day. A consistent routine encourages healthy habits, fosters emotional regulation, and allows you to feel grounded, even in the face of challenges.

As **Dr. John Ratey**, author of *Spark: The Revolutionary New Science of Exercise and the Brain*, states, "When we create structure in our lives, we are building a resilient foundation that allows us to thrive, not just survive" (Ratey, 2008). Routine provides the scaffolding for your recovery journey and helps you stay connected to your well-being.

The Components of a Healthy Routine

Creating a routine that supports your recovery involves addressing different areas of your life. A well-rounded routine balances physical health, emotional well-being, and social connection, while also leaving space for personal reflection and growth. Below are the key components of a healthy daily routine that can help support long-term sobriety and recovery:

1. **Morning Rituals to Start the Day Right**
   Starting your day with intention sets the tone for everything that follows. A morning routine can help you feel centered, grounded, and ready to face whatever challenges may come your way. This doesn't have to be complicated; even a few simple practices can help establish a positive start to your day.
   Ideas for Your Morning Routine:
   - Wake up at the same time each day to establish consistency.
   - Engage in mindful practices such as deep breathing, meditation, or gentle stretching.
   - Practice gratitude by listing three things you are thankful for.
   - Write in your journal to reflect on your thoughts and emotions.
   - Set a daily intention or goal, such as "Today, I will focus on staying grounded and compassionate toward myself."
2. **Exercise and Physical Activity**
   Physical activity is essential for both mental and physical health, especially in recovery. Regular exercise helps regulate mood, reduce

stress, and boost overall energy levels. It also provides a natural outlet for releasing any pent-up tension or frustration that can arise during recovery.

Ideas for Incorporating Exercise:

- Start your day with a short walk, yoga session, or stretching routine.
- Aim for at least 30 minutes of moderate exercise daily, such as swimming, jogging, or strength training.
- Consider joining a fitness class, running group, or local sports team for social engagement and support.
- Make exercise enjoyable—find activities that you genuinely like, whether it's dancing, cycling, or hiking.

Professional Insight:

"Exercise is a powerful tool for strengthening both the mind and body. It helps reduce stress and anxiety, improve sleep, and boost feelings of self-worth" – Dr. John Ratey, *Spark: The Revolutionary New Science of Exercise and the Brain* (Ratey, 2008).

3. **Nutrition and Hydration**

What you eat plays a significant role in how you feel physically and emotionally. A balanced diet helps stabilize blood sugar levels, maintain energy, and improve overall health. Proper hydration also supports mental clarity and physical well-being. Recovery is the perfect time to focus on nourishing your body with healthy, whole foods.

Ideas for Nutritional Wellness:

- Aim for balanced meals that include lean proteins, fruits, vegetables, whole grains, and healthy fats.

- Drink plenty of water throughout the day to stay hydrated and support brain function.
- Plan meals ahead of time to avoid making unhealthy food choices when you're hungry or stressed.
- Reduce caffeine and sugar intake, as these can contribute to anxiety, mood swings, or energy crashes.

Professional Insight:
"What we eat affects how we think, feel, and behave. Nutrition is an integral part of the recovery process, helping to heal both body and mind" – Dr. Drew Ramsey, author of *Eat Complete* (Ramsey, 2017).

4. **Work, Responsibilities, and Structure**

A healthy routine should include time for work, personal responsibilities, and productivity. Having structure around your daily tasks can give you a sense of purpose and accomplishment, which is vital for recovery. It also provides a framework that helps you stay engaged with your goals and avoid falling into the mental trap of boredom or isolation.

Ideas for Creating Structure in Your Day:

- Break your tasks into manageable chunks to avoid feeling overwhelmed.
- Use tools like planners, calendars, or productivity apps to stay organized.
- Prioritize your to-do list and focus on completing one task at a time.
- Schedule regular breaks throughout the day to avoid burnout.

Professional Insight:

"Structure provides the safety and predictability that we all need to feel secure. It helps to reduce stress and creates a sense of accomplishment" – Dr. Laura Schlessinger, author of *The Proper Care and Feeding of Marriage* (Schlessinger, 2005).

5. **Evening Rituals for Rest and Reflection**

Ending your day with intentional practices is just as important as starting it with intention. Evening rituals allow you to wind down, relax, and reflect on the events of the day. They can also improve the quality of your sleep, which is essential for your recovery.

Ideas for Your Evening Routine:

- Establish a consistent bedtime to ensure you're getting enough rest each night.
- Create a relaxing pre-bedtime routine, such as reading, meditating, or practicing deep breathing.
- Reflect on your day by journaling or simply reviewing what went well and what you're grateful for.
- Avoid stimulating activities, such as screen time, right before bed to promote restful sleep.

Professional Insight:

"Sleep is essential for recovery, both physical and emotional. Quality sleep restores your energy, reduces stress, and helps you maintain a clear and focused mind" – Dr. Matthew Walker, author of *Why We Sleep* (Walker, 2017).

Reflection Activity: Building Your Own Routine

Now that you've learned about the different components of a healthy routine, it's time to start building your own. Take a moment to reflect on your current daily habits and identify areas where you can add more structure or balance. Write down a simple, realistic routine that you can follow.

- **Morning Routine**:
- **Exercise Plan**:
- **Nutritional Goals**:
- **Work and Responsibility Schedule**:
- **Evening Wind-Down Rituals**:

Remember, your routine doesn't have to be perfect from the start. Begin with small steps and gradually build consistency over time. Flexibility is also important—life is unpredictable, and some days will be harder than others. But by committing to a healthy routine, you are creating the foundation for long-term success in recovery.

Exercise: Setting Your Intentions for the Day

Each morning, set one intention for your day. It could be as simple as practicing self-compassion or focusing on staying present. Write down your intention in your journal or on a sticky note and place it somewhere you will see it throughout the day.

- **Today's Intention:**
- **How I Will Stay Focused on This Intention:**

The Power of Routine in Recovery

A consistent, healthy routine can be one of the most effective tools in your recovery. It provides structure, reduces stress, and supports your physical, emotional, and mental well-being. By focusing on small, positive habits each day, you create a framework for long-term recovery success.

10

Finding and Nurturing Support Systems

The Importance of Support in Recovery

Recovery is not a solitary journey—it is a path that is enriched and supported by the people around you. One of the most crucial aspects of long-term sobriety is having a reliable support system. The challenges of recovery can be overwhelming at times, but having a network of people who understand your struggles, share your values, and encourage your growth can make all the difference.

Addiction often isolates individuals, leading to feelings of loneliness and disconnection. It's easy to believe that you must navigate recovery on your own. However, this mindset can be one of the biggest barriers to healing. Recovery is a collective process. It requires not only personal commitment but also the compassion, encouragement, and accountability of others.

Dr. Gabor Maté wisely says, "The opposite of addiction is not sobriety. The opposite of addiction is connection" (Maté, 2008). When you feel connected to others—whether through family, friends, support groups, or therapy—you are more likely to stay committed to your recovery. Human connection fosters emotional healing, reduces feelings of isolation, and builds resilience in the face of adversity.

Types of Support Systems in Recovery

There are many types of support systems you can cultivate in recovery. Each type plays a unique role in helping you stay grounded, encouraged, and accountable as you move through your journey.

1. **Family Support**
   Family can be one of the most important sources of support in recovery, but healing these relationships often takes time and effort. For families that have been affected by addiction, rebuilding trust and communication is essential. Family members may need their own healing as well, as they may have experienced their own pain and trauma due to the addiction.
   Tips for Rebuilding Family Support:
   - **Open communication**: Share your recovery journey with your family, allowing them to understand your progress and setbacks.
   - **Set boundaries**: Clearly communicate your needs, and respect the boundaries of others in the process.
   - **Seek family counseling**: Consider involving a therapist or counselor to guide family discussions and support healing.
2. **Peer Support**
   Peers who are also in recovery can offer a level of understanding and empathy that others may not be able to provide. Connecting with people who have walked a similar path can be immensely

comforting. Peer support groups like Alcoholics Anonymous (AA), Narcotics Anonymous (NA), or SMART Recovery provide a safe, judgment-free space where you can share your experiences, gain insight, and receive encouragement.

How to Connect with Peer Support:

- Attend 12-step meetings or other recovery support groups regularly.
- Engage in online or in-person forums for those in recovery.
- Find a sponsor or accountability partner to guide and support your journey.

Professional Insight:

"Support groups provide a community where members can share their struggles and triumphs, reinforcing the sense that recovery is possible and sustainable" – Dr. William R. Miller, author of *The Recovery Book* (Miller, 2006).

3. **Therapeutic Support**

Working with a therapist or counselor is an integral part of recovery. Therapy helps you process underlying emotions, identify root causes of addiction, and develop coping strategies for life's challenges. Individual therapy, group therapy, or family therapy all offer different avenues for support and healing.

How to Engage in Therapeutic Support:

- Commit to regular therapy sessions, either individually or in a group setting.

- Be open and honest with your therapist, allowing them to guide you through the deeper emotional work of recovery.
- Set recovery goals with your therapist and track your progress together.

4. **Community Support**

Beyond your immediate circle of family and friends, community support is also essential. This could include local or online recovery programs, spiritual communities, or social groups that align with your personal values. Finding a community of like-minded individuals can create a sense of belonging and purpose.

How to Build a Community of Support:

- Join a local or online recovery network or spiritual group that resonates with your values.
- Participate in social or recreational activities that promote health, well-being, and social engagement.
- Volunteer or give back to others in recovery, which can foster a sense of purpose and connection.

The Role of Vulnerability in Building Support

Building a support system requires vulnerability. For many individuals in recovery, the idea of reaching out for help can feel intimidating or uncomfortable. However, vulnerability is a key component of healing. It allows you to break down the walls of isolation and connect with others in an authentic way. By being open about your struggles, fears, and successes, you create deeper, more meaningful relationships.

Brené Brown, a researcher and expert on vulnerability, writes, "Vulnerability is not winning or losing; it's having the courage to show up and be seen when we have no control over the outcome" (Brown, 2012). Vulnerability is the foundation of trust and connection, and it's what allows your support system to grow and thrive.

Building Accountability Through Support

Accountability is one of the most important roles that a support system can provide. Having people in your life who hold you accountable for your recovery goals and actions can help you stay on track and motivated. Accountability partners—whether a sponsor, family member, or friend—can offer encouragement, check in on your progress, and provide gentle reminders when needed.

Here are some ways your support system can help with accountability:

- **Regular check-ins**: Schedule weekly or monthly check-ins with your accountability partner or sponsor.
- **Share your goals**: Clearly communicate your recovery goals with your support network so they can encourage and remind you of your progress.
- **Celebrate milestones**: Share your victories—both big and small—with your support system so that they can celebrate with you.

Self-Care Within Your Support System

While having a strong support system is crucial, it's also important to remember that your support network cannot replace your own self-care practices. You must prioritize your mental, physical, and emotional well-being, and this begins with self-compassion and boundaries. A healthy support system should uplift you without enabling unhealthy behaviors or draining your energy.

Take time for yourself—whether that's through meditation, therapy, exercise, or quiet reflection. By taking care of yourself, you'll be better equipped to support others and maintain strong, healthy relationships in recovery.

Reflection Activity: Identifying Your Support System

Reflect on the people and groups that currently make up your support system. Who in your life offers encouragement, understanding, and accountability? Write down the names of individuals or groups who provide positive support for your recovery.

- **Who are the people that support me in my recovery?**
- **What qualities make them a valuable part of my support system?**
- **Who else could I reach out to in my journey to strengthen my support network?**

Exercise: Reaching Out for Support

Reaching out for help is a powerful step in recovery. This exercise involves reaching out to someone in your support system, whether that's a friend, family member, or recovery group member. Share something positive about your progress or a challenge you're facing.

- **Today, I will reach out to [Name] and share...**
- **I will ask for support with [specific need or goal].**

The Healing Power of Connection

A strong support system can make all the difference in your recovery journey. By building relationships rooted in trust, honesty, and accountability, you create a safety net that supports your healing and growth. Remember, you don't have to walk this path alone. Whether it's family, friends, peers, or professionals, the people you surround yourself with will play an integral role in your recovery and the life you build beyond addiction.

11
: Staying Sober in Social Situations

The Challenge of Socializing in Recovery

Social situations can be both a source of joy and a challenge in recovery. On one hand, connecting with others and enjoying social activities is an important part of life and can promote a sense of community. On the other hand, socializing can be difficult when it brings you into environments or situations where substance use is present, or where old habits and triggers might resurface.

In recovery, it is essential to be proactive in how you approach social situations. Whether it's a family gathering, a party, or a casual night out with friends, maintaining your sobriety is possible with the right mindset, preparation, and coping strategies.

As **Dr. Mark S. Gold**, a leading addiction expert, writes: "The most important aspect of long-term recovery is learning to deal with everyday social situations that trigger addiction" (Gold, 2012). The ability to navigate social interactions while remaining true to your recovery goals is a skill that takes practice and self-awareness, but it is one that can be mastered.

Recognizing Triggers in Social Situations

Triggers are situations, people, or emotions that provoke the urge to use substances or engage in addictive behaviors. In social situations, triggers can be particularly challenging because they may involve past patterns of behavior, social pressure, or environments where substance use is the norm.

Here are some common triggers in social settings:

- **Being around people who are drinking or using substances**: This is one of the most common triggers, especially in the early stages of recovery.
- **Peer pressure or social norms**: Friends or family members may not understand your recovery journey, and their insistence on drinking or using substances can be difficult to resist.
- **Old habits or routines**: Socializing in the same places or with the same people that were once associated with substance use can provoke cravings.
- **Feelings of isolation or anxiety**: For many in recovery, social anxiety or fear of being judged in social settings can lead to stress, which might trigger the urge to cope through substances.

The first step in navigating social situations is to be aware of your triggers. By identifying what specifically might cause you to feel tempted, you can prepare yourself with strategies to manage these situations.

Strategies for Staying Sober in Social Situations

1. **Plan Ahead**

   One of the best ways to stay sober in social settings is to plan ahead.

This allows you to mentally prepare for the situation and decide on your course of action before you're faced with temptation.

How to Plan Ahead:

- **Set an intention**: Before entering any social situation, remind yourself of your recovery goals and why staying sober is important to you. Setting an intention can help you stay focused and grounded.
- **Have an exit strategy**: If you're entering a situation where you're unsure of the environment, have a plan for how you'll leave if it becomes uncomfortable or triggering. This can be as simple as having a trusted friend or sponsor you can call for support.
- **Practice saying no**: Be ready to politely decline offers to drink or use substances. Having a prepared response, such as, "I'm in recovery and don't drink," can make it easier to assert your boundaries.

2. **Create a Sober Social Network**

It's essential to surround yourself with people who respect your recovery and support your decision to stay sober. If possible, seek out social activities that don't involve alcohol or substance use.

Ideas for Sober Socializing:

- Attend recovery support group meetings or social events specifically for those in recovery.
- Engage in sober activities, such as hiking, attending a movie, or cooking dinner with friends.
- Find a recovery buddy—someone who shares your commitment to sobriety and can attend social gatherings with you for mutual support.

Professional Insight:
"The people we surround ourselves with can either support or hinder our recovery journey. It's important to build a sober support system and engage in activities that reinforce our commitment to sobriety" – Dr. William Miller, *The Recovery Book* (Miller, 2006).

3. **Stay Focused on Your Recovery Goals**

When you're in social situations, it can be easy to lose sight of your recovery goals, especially when you feel pressure or temptation. Keep your goals at the forefront of your mind and remind yourself of the reasons why you're committed to staying sober.

How to Stay Focused:

- **Carry a reminder**: Have a token, an affirmation, or a small note with you that reminds you of your commitment to recovery. This could be something like a medallion, a note on your phone, or a mantra you repeat to yourself when faced with temptation.
- **Use mindful awareness**: When you're feeling triggered, use mindfulness techniques such as deep breathing or grounding exercises to stay present and focused on your goals.

4. **Limit Your Time in High-Risk Environments**

While it's important to challenge yourself in recovery, it's also important to recognize your limits. If you're in an environment that is overwhelming or high-risk for relapse, it may be best to limit your time in that setting. Gradually expose yourself to social situations as you build more confidence in your ability to maintain your sobriety.

How to Navigate High-Risk Environments:

- If you're in a situation where others are drinking or using substances, find ways to remove yourself or stay in a safe space within the setting.
- Bring a supportive friend who understands your recovery and can help you navigate the situation.
- Take a break if needed—stepping outside or finding a quiet corner to regroup can help you regain control of the situation.

The Importance of Boundaries

Setting and respecting boundaries is crucial when navigating social situations. Boundaries protect your emotional well-being and help you maintain your sobriety, particularly when interacting with people who may not fully understand your recovery journey.

Here are some key boundary-setting strategies:

- **Know when to say no**: You are not obligated to attend every social event or gathering, especially if you know it will be triggering. It's okay to decline invitations or leave early if you feel uncomfortable.
- **Be clear about your needs**: Let others know that you are in recovery and may need to avoid certain situations or environments. Respectfully communicate your boundaries with friends and family so they can support your choices.
- **Avoid enabling behaviors**: Be mindful of relationships where others may encourage unhealthy behaviors or enable your past habits. Setting boundaries in these relationships helps protect your recovery and well-being.

Reflection Activity: Your Social Support Plan

Take a moment to reflect on the social situations you find most challenging. Identify the potential triggers and plan for how you will handle them in a healthy way. Write down your strategies for maintaining sobriety in these situations.

- **What are my common social triggers?**
- **How will I handle situations where substances are present?**
- **Who can I rely on for support when I'm in a social setting?**

Exercise: Creating a Sober Activity List

Create a list of activities that you enjoy and that don't involve substances. These can be fun and meaningful alternatives to social events where substances are present. Share this list with a trusted friend or recovery buddy, and plan to engage in one of these activities regularly.

- **Sober Activities I Enjoy:**
    - Hiking
    - Yoga or fitness classes
    - Cooking or baking
    - Attending art classes or creative workshops
    - Volunteering
    - Going to the movies or museums

Finding Strength in Socializing Sober

Staying sober in social situations is an ongoing practice that requires awareness, preparation, and commitment. With the right strategies in place, you can enjoy socializing and connecting with others without compromising your recovery. Remember that you have the power to set boundaries, make conscious choices, and seek support when needed. Your recovery is worth protecting, and every successful social interaction is a victory on your path to healing.

12

Developing a Relapse Prevention Plan

The Importance of Relapse Prevention

In recovery, relapse is a real and often unavoidable challenge. While it can feel like a setback, relapse is not the end of the road; it is an opportunity to learn, grow, and adjust your approach to recovery. Developing a relapse prevention plan is essential because it helps you anticipate potential challenges, recognize early warning signs, and take proactive steps to prevent relapse from occurring.

Dr. Patrick Carnes, a leading expert in addiction, writes, "Relapse is a process, not an event" (Carnes, 2005). This means that relapse doesn't typically happen all at once—it unfolds gradually as small decisions, behaviors, or emotional triggers build up over time. A well-developed prevention plan helps you recognize these warning signs early and take action to protect your sobriety.

In this chapter, we'll explore how to create a personalized relapse prevention plan, identify your triggers, and develop strategies for managing cravings and high-risk situations. With a solid plan in place, you'll be better equipped to navigate the challenges of recovery and stay focused on your long-term goals.

Identifying Your Triggers

Triggers are the specific situations, people, emotions, or environments that can lead to cravings or the urge to use substances. Identifying your triggers is the first step in preventing relapse. By recognizing the factors that influence your behavior, you can prepare for these situations and make intentional choices that support your recovery.

Triggers can be both **external** and **internal**:

- **External Triggers**: These are external situations or people that prompt the desire to use substances. Examples include being around others who are drinking or using drugs, visiting places where you previously used, or encountering high-stress situations like conflict or pressure.
- **Internal Triggers**: These are emotional or psychological states that drive the urge to use. Examples include feelings of anger, anxiety, depression, loneliness, or boredom.

Dr. Gabor Maté says, "Addiction is not about the substance or the behavior; it is a response to emotional pain" (Maté, 2008). Understanding both your external and internal triggers allows you to take steps to avoid or cope with them in healthy ways.

Developing Coping Strategies for Triggers

Once you've identified your triggers, the next step is developing strategies to manage them when they arise. Coping strategies are essential for staying sober, especially when you are faced with difficult situations or emotions.

Here are some coping strategies that can help you navigate triggers:

1. **Mindfulness and Grounding Techniques**

Mindfulness practices, such as deep breathing and body awareness, help you stay present and reduce the intensity of cravings. Grounding exercises, such as the 5-4-3-2-1 technique (naming things you can see, hear, feel, etc.), help you reconnect with the present moment and distract your mind from cravings.

How to Practice:

- When you notice a craving or a trigger, pause and take a few deep breaths.
- Use grounding techniques to re-center yourself and bring your focus back to your environment.
- Remind yourself that cravings are temporary and will pass.

2. **Developing Healthy Distractions**

Finding activities that distract you from cravings can be an effective way to prevent relapse. Distractions can be anything that takes your mind off the craving, whether it's engaging in a hobby, going for a walk, or reaching out to a support person.

How to Practice:

- Create a list of healthy distractions that you enjoy—exercise, journaling, calling a friend, working on a creative project, etc.
- Keep this list handy so that when cravings arise, you can immediately turn to a healthy distraction.

3. **Building a Support Network**

One of the most effective ways to prevent relapse is to build a strong support system. Having people you can turn to when you're struggling can make all the difference. Whether it's a sponsor, a therapist, or a group of friends who support your sobriety, leaning on others can help you stay grounded and accountable.

How to Practice:

- Reach out to your support system when you feel triggered or tempted.
- Attend recovery meetings regularly to stay connected to others who understand your journey.
- Share your struggles with a trusted individual so you don't have to face them alone.

4. **Creating an Emergency Plan**

It's important to have an emergency plan in place in case you find yourself in a high-risk situation. This plan should outline specific steps to take if you feel like you're at risk of relapse.

How to Create Your Emergency Plan:

- Identify the people you can call for support (sponsor, therapist, recovery buddy).
- Have a list of healthy coping strategies you can implement when cravings arise.
- Know when to leave a situation if it's unsafe or triggering.
- Practice self-compassion—remember that setbacks are part of the process, not a failure.

Setting Realistic Goals for Recovery

In order to prevent relapse, it's important to set clear, achievable goals that keep you focused on your long-term recovery. These goals should be realistic and broken down into smaller, manageable steps.

How to Set Goals:

- **Short-Term Goals**: These could include daily or weekly objectives, such as attending meetings, practicing self-care, or reaching out to a support person.
- **Long-Term Goals**: These could focus on milestones in your recovery journey, such as achieving 6 months or a year of sobriety, building new healthy habits, or repairing relationships.

By setting both short-term and long-term goals, you create a roadmap for your recovery that keeps you focused and motivated.

Reflection Activity: Identifying Your Personal Triggers and Coping Strategies

Take time to reflect on your personal triggers and the strategies that can help you manage them. This exercise will help you develop a personalized relapse prevention plan that fits your unique needs.

My External Triggers:

My Internal Triggers:

My Coping Strategies:

My Support Network:

My Emergency Plan:

Exercise: Creating a Relapse Prevention Plan

Now that you've identified your triggers and coping strategies, it's time to create your relapse prevention plan. Write down the following steps you will take to stay sober and maintain your recovery:

1. **I will recognize and address my triggers by...**
2. **I will implement the following coping strategies when cravings arise...**
3. **I will stay connected to my support network by...**
4. **I will commit to my recovery by...**

Having a written plan makes it easier to follow through when faced with challenges. Keep your plan in a place where you can refer to it when needed.

The Power of Resilience in Recovery

Relapse is a part of many people's recovery journey, but it does not define who you are or how far you've come. Developing a solid relapse prevention plan can help you build the resilience needed to face challenges and setbacks with strength and confidence. Remember, each day is an opportunity to move forward in your recovery, and you have the tools and support to continue on your path toward healing.

13

Setting and Achieving Long-Term Goals

The Role of Goals in Recovery

Setting goals is a powerful tool in recovery. Goals give you direction, focus, and something to work toward. They provide a sense of purpose and accomplishment, which is essential for maintaining motivation and momentum in your journey. In recovery, goals help you measure progress, stay accountable, and create a future that aligns with your values and desires.

As **Dr. Viktor Frankl**, a renowned psychiatrist and Holocaust survivor, once said, "Those who have a why to live, can bear almost any how" (Frankl, 1946). In other words, having a clear vision of your future and understanding why your recovery matters can give you the strength to face challenges, setbacks, and temptations.

In this chapter, we'll explore how to set long-term goals in recovery, stay motivated, and create a plan to achieve those goals. With the right tools and mindset, you can not only stay sober but build a meaningful, fulfilling life after addiction.

The Power of Long-Term Goals

Long-term goals are the big dreams that fuel your recovery journey. They represent the future you are working to create—whether it's rebuilding relationships, pursuing a career, or finding peace within yourself. These goals are your "why" for recovery; they give your journey meaning and purpose beyond just staying sober.

However, long-term goals can sometimes feel distant or overwhelming, especially when you're still early in recovery. It's important to break these larger goals down into smaller, more manageable steps. That way, each step feels achievable and you can celebrate progress along the way.

Dr. William Miller, in his work on motivation and change, states, "Change is not easy, but it is possible. Setting goals and committing to them is a critical part of that change process" (Miller, 2006). The act of setting and working toward goals is an essential part of the transformation that happens in recovery.

Creating Your Long-Term Vision

A crucial first step in setting long-term goals is to create a vision for your life beyond addiction. What does your ideal future look like? What kind of person do you want to become, and what do you want to accomplish? This vision will guide your actions and decisions as you move through recovery.

Here are some prompts to help you create your long-term vision:

- **How do you want your life to look in 1 year, 3 years, or 5 years?**
- **What kind of relationships do you want to build with family and friends?**

- **What passions, hobbies, or career goals do you want to pursue?**
- **What kind of health—mental, emotional, and physical—do you want to experience?**
- **How do you want to feel in your own skin? What emotional healing do you hope to achieve?**

Taking time to create this vision helps clarify what recovery truly means to you. It becomes a guiding light for the decisions you make each day.

Setting SMART Goals

Once you have a vision for your life, the next step is setting SMART goals to make that vision a reality. SMART goals are specific, measurable, achievable, relevant, and time-bound. These types of goals are designed to be clear and actionable, so you can stay focused on what's most important.

SMART Goals:

- **Specific**: Clearly define what you want to accomplish.
- **Measurable**: Make sure the goal is quantifiable so you can track your progress.
- **Achievable**: Set a goal that is realistic, taking into account your current circumstances.
- **Relevant**: Choose goals that are meaningful and aligned with your values and vision.
- **Time-bound**: Set a timeline or deadline to keep yourself accountable.

Example of a SMART Goal:

- **Goal**: "I will attend three therapy sessions a month for the next six months to work on emotional healing and self-compassion."
- **Specific**: Attending therapy sessions.
- **Measurable**: Three sessions per month.
- **Achievable**: Based on current availability and commitment.
- **Relevant**: Emotional healing is important for recovery.
- **Time-bound**: For the next six months.

By breaking down larger goals into smaller, manageable steps, you create a roadmap that makes progress feel tangible and attainable.

Staying Motivated in Recovery

Maintaining motivation can be challenging, especially when the initial excitement of recovery starts to fade, or when you face difficult emotions or situations. It's normal to experience periods of doubt or fatigue, but staying connected to your goals can reignite your motivation and keep you on track.

Here are a few ways to stay motivated:

- **Celebrate Small Wins**: Recognize and celebrate the progress you make, even in small increments. Each step forward is a victory, and acknowledging these wins boosts your confidence and keeps you motivated.
- **Reconnect with Your Why**: Whenever you feel discouraged, remind yourself of why you started this journey in the first place. What does recovery mean to you? Reconnect with your long-term vision and let it reignite your passion.

- **Track Your Progress**: Keep a journal or tracker to record your achievements and challenges. Seeing how far you've come can provide the encouragement you need to keep going.
- **Visualize Your Future**: Use visualization techniques to imagine yourself achieving your long-term goals. This can reinforce the belief that your dreams are achievable and motivate you to take consistent action.
- **Stay Flexible**: Life is unpredictable, and there will be times when things don't go as planned. Stay flexible and adjust your goals when necessary, but always keep moving forward. Remember that setbacks are part of the process, not the end.

Professional Insight:

"Recovery is a marathon, not a sprint. Setting long-term goals and maintaining motivation are key to staying committed through the ups and downs" – Dr. William Miller, *The Recovery Book* (Miller, 2006).

Reflection Activity: Your Long-Term Vision

Take time to reflect on your long-term goals and what you want your life to look like in the future. Write down your vision and break it down into specific, actionable steps.

- **My Long-Term Vision for Recovery:**
- **What do I want to accomplish in the next 1 year, 3 years, and 5 years?**
- **What small goals can I set to help me move toward this vision?**
- **What resources or support will I need to achieve these goals?**

Exercise: SMART Goal Setting

Think about a key area of your life that you want to improve or accomplish. Set a SMART goal for this area and create a timeline for when you want to achieve it.

- **Goal Area (e.g., career, relationships, health, emotional well-being):**
- **Specific Goal:**
- **Measurable Outcome:**
- **Achievable Steps:**
- **Timeline:**
- **How I will track my progress:**

The Journey Forward

Setting long-term goals and staying motivated in recovery is not just about maintaining sobriety—it's about creating a life that is fulfilling, meaningful, and rich with possibilities. By setting clear, achievable goals and staying committed to them, you are laying the foundation for a future beyond addiction. Remember, recovery is a lifelong journey, and every day is an opportunity to move closer to the person you are meant to be.

This concludes the workbook. You've now developed a plan for your journey forward, with tools, strategies, and insights to guide you along the way. Recovery is possible, and you are capable of achieving your goals—one step at a time.

Summary

Ember of Hope: Kindling the Flame of Recovery has guided you through the essential aspects of recovery, providing tools, strategies, and insights to support your healing journey. Throughout this workbook, we've explored the importance of self-compassion, building a solid support system, setting goals, and understanding the role of trauma in addiction. Each chapter offered practical exercises and reflective activities to help you develop the emotional resilience needed to navigate the challenges of recovery.

In recovery, there will be moments of difficulty, but each step you take forward is a step toward a healthier, more fulfilling life. The coping strategies, mindfulness practices, and goal-setting techniques shared here are designed to empower you to stay grounded and focused on your long-term vision, while also providing the flexibility to adjust and adapt to the evolving nature of your journey.

Recovery is a lifelong process. It requires patience, self-compassion, and the courage to face your inner truths. With the tools provided in this workbook, you are well-equipped to continue on your path toward healing and growth, knowing that each day offers new opportunities for self-discovery and transformation.

Acknowledgements

This workbook would not have been possible without the inspiration and support of many people. To the countless individuals in recovery who shared their stories, struggles, and triumphs, thank you for your courage and vulnerability. Your experiences have shaped the very foundation of this work.

I would like to express my deepest gratitude to the professionals, mentors, and recovery advocates whose knowledge and expertise have informed the principles shared in this book. Your dedication to helping others heal and grow is truly remarkable.

A special thank you to my family and friends, whose unwavering love and encouragement have been a constant source of strength. Your support has been essential in helping me stay committed to my work and to this project.

To all the clinicians, therapists, and addiction specialists who provide care and guidance to those in need: Your work is life-changing, and I honor the compassion and dedication you bring to your clients each day.

Finally, to you, the reader, thank you for allowing me to walk alongside you in this phase of your journey. Your commitment to recovery is an act of immense courage, and I am grateful to have been a part of it. Remember, you are not alone, and healing is always possible.

Helpful Resources and Recommended Books

Books on Recovery and Addiction

- *The Recovery Book: Answers to All Your Questions About Addiction and Alcoholism* by William R. Miller (2006)
- *Out of the Shadows: Understanding Sexual Addiction* by Patrick Carnes (2005)
- *In the Realm of Hungry Ghosts: Close Encounters with Addiction* by Gabor Maté (2008)
- *Addiction Recovery Management: Theory, Research, and Practice* by Mark S. Gold (2012)
- *Man's Search for Meaning* by Viktor E. Frankl (1946)
- *The Gifts of Imperfection: Let Go of Who You Think You're Supposed to Be and Embrace Who You Are* by Brené Brown (2008)

Books on Mindfulness and Emotional Regulation

- *Full Catastrophe Living: Using the Wisdom of Your Body and Mind to Face Stress, Pain, and Illness* by Jon Kabat-Zinn (1990)
- *The Body Keeps the Score: Brain, Mind, and Body in the Healing of Trauma* by Bessel van der Kolk (2014)
- *The Power of Now: A Guide to Spiritual Enlightenment* by Eckhart Tolle (1997)

Books on Therapy and Treatment for Trauma

- *Betrayal Trauma: The Logic of Forgetting Childhood Abuse* by Jennifer J. Freyd (1996)
- *Cognitive-Behavioral Treatment of Borderline Personality Disorder* by Marsha M. Linehan (1993)
- *Opening Up: The Healing Power of Expressing Emotions* by James W. Pennebaker (1997)

Books on Health, Wellness, and Nutrition

- *Eat Complete: The 21 Nutrients That Fuel Brainpower, Boost Weight Loss, and Transform Your Health* by Drew Ramsey (2017)
- *Why We Sleep: Unlocking the Power of Sleep and Dreams* by Matthew Walker (2017)
- *Spark: The Revolutionary New Science of Exercise and the Brain* by John Ratey (2008)
- *Spontaneous Healing: How to Discover and Enhance Your Body's Natural Ability to Maintain and Heal Itself* by Andrew Weil (1995)

Support Groups and Websites

- **Alcoholics Anonymous (AA)**: https://www.aa.org
- **Narcotics Anonymous (NA)**: https://www.na.org
- **SMART Recovery**: https://www.smartrecovery.org
- **The National Institute on Drug Abuse (NIDA)**: https://www.drugabuse.gov
- **Substance Abuse and Mental Health Services Administration (SAMHSA)**: https://www.samhsa.gov

Therapy and Counseling Resources

- **Psychology Today Therapist Directory**: https://www.psychologytoday.com
- **Therapist Finder (GoodTherapy)**: https://www.goodtherapy.org

References

Brown, B. (2008). *The gifts of imperfection: Let go of who you think you're supposed to be and embrace who you are*. Hazelden Publishing.

Carnes, P. (2005). *Out of the shadows: Understanding sexual addiction*. Hazelden Publishing.

Cloud, H. (1992). *Boundaries: When to say yes, how to say no to take control of your life*. Zondervan.

Covington, S. (2008). *Women and addiction: A gender-responsive approach*. Journal of Psychoactive Drugs, 40(1), 13-16.

Freyd, J. J. (1996). *Betrayal trauma: The logic of forgetting childhood abuse*. Harvard University Press.

Frankl, V. E. (1946). *Man's search for meaning*. Beacon Press.

Gold, M. S. (2012). *Addiction recovery management: Theory, research, and practice*. Springer Science & Business Media.

Kabat-Zinn, J. (1990). *Full catastrophe living: Using the wisdom of your body and mind to face stress, pain, and illness*. Delta.

Linehan, M. M. (1993). *Cognitive-behavioral treatment of borderline personality disorder*. Guilford Press.

Miller, W. R. (2006). *The recovery book: Answers to all your questions about addiction and alcoholic recovery*. Hachette Books.

Maté, G. (2008). *In the realm of hungry ghosts: Close encounters with addiction*. North Atlantic Books.

Pennebaker, J. W. (1997). *Opening up: The healing power of expressing emotions*. Guilford Press.

Ratey, J. J. (2008). *Spark: The revolutionary new science of exercise and the brain*. Little, Brown Spark.

Ramsey, D. (2017). *Eat complete: The 21 nutrients that fuel brainpower, boost weight loss, and transform your health*. Workman Publishing.

Schlessinger, L. (2005). *The proper care and feeding of marriage*. HarperCollins.

van der Kolk, B. (2014). *The body keeps the score: Brain, mind, and body in the healing of trauma*. Viking.

Walker, M. (2017). *Why we sleep: Unlocking the power of sleep and dreams*. Scribner.

Weil, A. (1995). *Spontaneous healing: How to discover and enhance your body's natural ability to maintain and heal itself*. Knopf.

www.ingramcontent.com/pod-product-compliance
Lightning Source LLC
La Vergne TN
LVHW090329210926
848480LV00004B/1345